Table of Contents

Introduction

Welcome to "The Ultimate Guide on How to Start a Pop-up Restaurant"! If you've ever dreamed of owning a restaurant, but the idea of a permanent location seems daunting, or if you're an experienced entrepreneur looking to try something new, then you're in the right place. This book is your comprehensive guide to the exciting world of pop-up restaurants. Whether you're a food enthusiast with a culinary vision or a business owner seeking a fresh venture, we're here to provide you with the knowledge and tools you need to launch your own pop-up restaurant successfully.

Pop-up restaurants have been gaining traction in recent years, and for good reason. These temporary dining experiences offer a unique and innovative way to connect with customers. They allow you to showcase your culinary creativity and test out your ideas without the long-term commitment of a permanent establishment. With the right planning and execution, a pop-up restaurant can create buzz, generate revenue, and even pave the way for a permanent spot in the culinary world.

Throughout this book, we'll cover every aspect of starting a pop-up restaurant. We'll start by helping you assess your concept and vision, ensuring you understand what makes your restaurant unique in a competitive market. This is crucial because your concept will be the foundation of your entire venture. From there, we'll guide you through the process of planning your menu and recipes, making sure they not only reflect your culinary expertise but also resonate with your target audience.

Location is another critical factor in the success of any restaurant. We'll provide insights into finding the perfect spot for your pop-up, considering factors like foot traffic, ambiance, and accessibility. Additionally, navigating the legal and regulatory landscape is essential for any food establishment, and pop-ups are no exception. We'll help you understand the necessary permits and regulations to ensure you operate smoothly and confidently.

Marketing and promotion are vital for attracting customers to your pop-up restaurant. We'll share innovative ideas and effective techniques to create awareness, build anticipation, and drive traffic to your establishment. From social media strategies to local partnerships, we'll cover it all. Staffing and operations are equally important, and we'll offer tips on assembling a reliable team and streamlining your daily processes to ensure a seamless operation.

Creating an unforgettable dining experience is key to standing out in the competitive restaurant industry. We'll explore various elements that can elevate your pop-up, such as ambiance, customer service, and even the little details like table settings. These aspects can leave a lasting impression on your guests and turn first-time visitors into loyal customers.

Financial management and budgeting are crucial for the sustainability and profitability of your business. We'll guide you through effective financial strategies, helping you make informed decisions and maintain a healthy bottom line. We'll also discuss how to evaluate the success of your pop-up restaurant and explore future opportunities for growth and expansion.

Are you ready to embark on this exciting journey into the world of pop-up restaurants? Let's dive in and uncover the key steps and strategies to turn your pop-up dream into a reality. With passion, creativity, and a little guidance from this book, you'll be well on your way to creating a memorable and successful pop-up restaurant.

Chapter 1: Introduction to Pop-Up Restaurants

Pop-up restaurants have taken the culinary world by storm, becoming a hot trend that everyone seems to be talking about. These temporary dining spots offer a unique and thrilling experience that draws in food lovers and curious diners alike. In this chapter, we're going to dive into the concept of pop-up restaurants and explore why they've become such a hit in recent years.

What is a Pop-Up Restaurant?

So, what exactly is a pop-up restaurant? Often referred to as supper clubs or guerrilla dining, these are temporary dining spaces that operate for a limited period, typically anywhere from a few days to a few months. Pop-ups can take many shapes and forms: some might take over an existing restaurant during off-peak hours, while others might set up in unusual places like warehouses, rooftops, or even vacant storefronts.

The magic of pop-up restaurants lies in their fleeting existence. They bring a sense of exclusivity and excitement, appearing and disappearing almost like culinary mirages. This transient nature creates a buzz, drawing in food enthusiasts eager to experience something out of the ordinary. Pop-ups often feature unique themes, innovative menus, and immersive dining experiences that you just can't find in traditional restaurants.

The Benefits of Starting a Pop-Up Restaurant

Starting a pop-up restaurant comes with several perks. Here are some key benefits:

1. **Low Initial Investment**: Compared to opening a traditional brick-and-mortar restaurant, pop-ups require much less upfront capital. This makes them an attractive option for aspiring restaurateurs who want to test their ideas without committing to a long-term lease or costly renovations.
2. **Flexibility and Creativity**: Pop-ups are a playground for creativity. Chefs and entrepreneurs can experiment with new concepts, cuisines, and dining formats. The temporary nature allows for greater flexibility in menu development and overall restaurant design.
3. **Building Brand Awareness**: A pop-up restaurant can generate significant buzz and help build a strong following. It provides a platform for chefs and restaurateurs to showcase their talents, establish their brand identity, and attract attention from both food lovers and media outlets.
4. **Testing the Market**: Pop-ups are a fantastic way to test new restaurant concepts. They allow you to gauge customer preferences, gather feedback, and

make necessary adjustments before committing to a permanent venture.

Challenges of Running a Pop-Up Restaurant

While pop-up restaurants offer numerous benefits, they're not without their challenges. Here are a few you might encounter:

1. **Limited Timeframe:** The temporary nature of pop-ups means you have a limited window to generate revenue and establish your brand. This requires careful planning and efficient execution to make the most of your time.
2. **Finding Suitable Locations:** Securing the perfect location for a pop-up can be tricky. You'll need to research and negotiate with landlords or property owners to find available spaces that match your concept and target audience.
3. **Managing Logistics:** Running a pop-up involves juggling various logistical aspects, like obtaining permits, sourcing equipment, hiring staff, and managing inventory. Good organization and coordination are crucial to ensure smooth operations.
4. **Marketing and Promotion:** Because pop-ups are short-lived, effective marketing and promotion are vital. You'll need to come up with innovative strategies to create awareness, generate excitement, and drive foot traffic to your pop-up.

In the chapters that follow, we'll dive deeper into each aspect of starting and running a pop-up restaurant. We'll provide you with the knowledge and guidance you need to embark on this exciting culinary adventure. So, get ready to learn all about how to make your pop-up restaurant a smashing success!

Chapter 2: Assessing Your Concept and Vision

So, you're thinking about starting a pop-up restaurant? That's exciting! Before you dive into the details, it's important to assess your concept and vision. This step is crucial because it helps you brainstorm and refine your ideas to create a unique and successful dining experience. Let's break it down into a few key areas: identifying your target audience, defining your brand identity, and conducting market research. Ready? Let's get started!

Identify Your Target Audience

First things first, you need to figure out who you're cooking for. Who are the people you want to attract to your pop-up restaurant? Understanding the demographics, preferences, and dining habits of your potential customers will help you tailor your concept and menu to their tastes.

Are you aiming to attract young professionals, families, or food enthusiasts? Think about the people in your chosen location. Are they looking for trendy new dining experiences or something more family-friendly? Consider factors like cuisine, ambiance, and price range. For example, young professionals might appreciate a chic, modern vibe with innovative dishes, while families might prefer a cozy, welcoming atmosphere with comfort food options.

Define Your Brand Identity

Your brand identity is what will make your pop-up restaurant stand out from the crowd. It's not just about a catchy name and a cool logo, although those are important too. It's about the whole experience you offer. Take some time to think about the atmosphere you want to create and the emotions you want your customers to feel when they dine with you.

Are you going for a casual and trendy vibe, or are you aiming for something more upscale and sophisticated? Your brand identity will influence your menu, decor, and marketing efforts. For instance, if you want a relaxed, hipster feel, you might choose rustic decor and a menu full of comfort foods with a modern twist. On the other hand, if you're going for elegance, your decor might be sleek and minimalistic, with a menu featuring gourmet dishes.

Conduct Market Research

To set your pop-up restaurant up for success, you need to do your homework. This means conducting thorough market research. Gather information about your target market, competitors, and current industry trends.

Start by looking at local demand for your type of cuisine. Are people in your area craving what you have to offer? Then, check out the competition.

Who are the other players in the market, and what are they doing well? Understanding the market landscape will help you make informed decisions about your concept, menu, pricing, and overall positioning.

Refine Your Menu

With a clear understanding of your target audience and brand identity, it's time to get creative with your menu. Think about the type of cuisine that fits your concept and will appeal to your target market. Your menu should be a balance of popular dishes and unique creations that showcase your culinary skills.

Keep in mind the logistical constraints of a pop-up restaurant. Your menu needs to be something you can prepare efficiently without compromising on quality. For instance, you might want to include a few signature dishes that are easy to make but pack a punch in terms of flavor and presentation.

Consider Collaborations and Themes

Adding a unique twist to your pop-up restaurant can really make it shine. One way to do this is through collaborations. Partnering with other local businesses or chefs can create buzz and attract a wider audience. For example, you could team up with a local brewery for a beer and food pairing event or join forces with a renowned pastry chef for a dessert-focused pop-up.

Themes can also enhance the dining experience. Think about incorporating a specific culinary region, a seasonal theme, or highlighting a particular ingredient. A well-executed theme can make your pop-up restaurant memorable and exciting for your guests.

Conclusion

Assessing your concept and vision is a vital step in starting your pop-up restaurant. By identifying your target audience, defining your brand identity, conducting thorough market research, and refining your menu, you'll lay a solid foundation for a unique and enticing dining experience. When you have a clear understanding of your concept and vision, you'll be ready to create a remarkable pop-up restaurant that stands out in the market. So, take your time with this step, and get ready to wow your future guests!

Chapter 3: Planning Your Menu and Recipes

Planning your menu and recipes is one of the most exciting and crucial steps in creating a successful pop-up restaurant. Your menu isn't just a list of dishes—it's the heart and soul of your dining experience, and it plays a significant role in attracting and satisfying your target audience. Let's dive into the key considerations and steps to develop an exceptional menu for your pop-up restaurant.

Understanding Your Target Audience

Before you start crafting your menu, it's essential to understand your target audience deeply. Think about their preferences, dietary restrictions, and culinary expectations. Conducting market research and gathering feedback from potential customers can be incredibly helpful in this process. Who are your diners? What do they love to eat? What are their dining habits?

Consider the demographics, lifestyle, and dining habits of your audience. Are they adventurous eaters who love trying new flavors, or do they prefer classic, comfort foods? Are they health-conscious, or do they enjoy indulging in rich, decadent dishes? By understanding their preferences, you can tailor your menu to meet their expectations and create a dining experience they'll remember.

Defining Your Concept and Brand Identity

Your menu should be a reflection of your concept and brand identity. Think about the atmosphere and overall theme of your pop-up restaurant. Is it a cozy, rustic spot with a focus on farm-to-table ingredients, or a sleek, modern space showcasing innovative culinary techniques? Your menu should complement these elements and enhance the overall dining experience.

Develop a culinary concept that sets you apart from other restaurants. This could be a unique fusion of cuisines, a focus on local and seasonal ingredients, or a specific cooking technique that you're passionate about. Your concept should not only reflect your culinary expertise but also resonate with your target audience.

Curating the Menu

When planning your menu, aim for a balance between creativity and feasibility. It's important to showcase your culinary skills while also considering the operational constraints of a pop-up restaurant. Start by selecting a few standout dishes that will be the stars of your menu. These dishes should be unique, delicious, and representative of your concept.

From there, build a complementary selection of appetizers, entrees, desserts, and beverages.

Consider offering options for different dietary preferences and restrictions, such as vegetarian, vegan, or gluten-free dishes. Ensure that your menu items can be executed efficiently within the limitations of your pop-up setup. Take into account the equipment, space, and time available to you. It's essential to choose recipes that can be prepared quickly without compromising on quality.

The Power of Specials and Seasonality

One of the best ways to keep your menu fresh and exciting is through daily or weekly specials. This allows you to experiment with new dishes and ingredients, creating a sense of anticipation for your customers. Incorporating seasonal produce into your menu can also add a touch of freshness and highlight local flavors.

Consider collaborating with local suppliers, farmers, or artisans to source high-quality and unique ingredients. This not only adds a distinct flavor to your dishes but also supports local businesses and adds to the authenticity of your pop-up restaurant.

Presenting Your Menu

Once you've finalized your menu, pay close attention to its presentation. A well-designed and organized menu can enhance the dining experience and entice customers. Consider using visually appealing descriptions, mouthwatering imagery, and clear categorizations for easy navigation. Utilize your brand identity in designing your menu's format and layout. Ensure that your menu reflects the overall aesthetic of your pop-up restaurant, creating a cohesive and memorable experience for your customers.

Conclusion

Planning your menu and recipes is a creative and essential aspect of starting a pop-up restaurant. By understanding your target audience, defining your concept, curating a balanced menu, embracing specials and seasonality, and presenting your menu effectively, you can create a remarkable dining experience that leaves a lasting impression on your customers. Remember to continuously refine and adapt your menu based on customer feedback and changing trends in the culinary world.

Are you ready to start planning your menu? Let's take this exciting step together and create something truly special for your pop-up restaurant!

Chapter 4: Finding the Right Location

Finding the perfect location for your pop-up restaurant is absolutely crucial. The right spot can make a huge difference in how your guests experience your restaurant and can greatly impact the visibility and profitability of your business. In this chapter, we're going to explore the key considerations and strategies for finding that ideal location.

Understanding Your Target Audience and Concept

Before you even start looking for a location, it's essential to have a clear understanding of your target audience and concept. Think about the demographics, preferences, and habits of the people you want to attract. Are they more likely to visit a particular neighborhood or area? Do they prefer certain types of venues or atmospheres?

For instance, if you're aiming for a trendy and hip crowd, you'll want to focus on areas with a vibrant food scene and a younger demographic. On the other hand, if your concept is more upscale and refined, you might want to consider neighborhoods with a higher income demographic. Understanding these factors will help you narrow down potential locations that align with your concept and brand identity.

Researching Potential Locations

Once you have a solid grasp of your target audience and concept, it's time to start researching potential locations. Here are a few strategies to help you in your search:

1. **Scout Different Neighborhoods**: Take the time to visit various neighborhoods and explore their dining scenes. Pay close attention to foot traffic, nearby attractions, and the overall vibe of the area. Look for spots that align with your target audience and concept.

2. **Collaborate with Other Businesses**: Partnering with existing businesses can be a fantastic way to find a space for your pop-up restaurant. This could be a café, bar, or any establishment with a compatible concept. Such collaborations can benefit both parties by attracting new customers and creating a unique experience.

3. **Utilize Online Platforms**: There are several online platforms and directories that connect businesses with available spaces for rent. Websites like ShareDinings, Popertunity, and Storefront allow you to search for temporary spaces that can be perfect for pop-up restaurants.

4. **Consider Non-Traditional Locations**: Pop-up restaurants are known for their creativity and uniqueness. Think outside the box when it comes to finding a location. It could be a rooftop, a garden, a repurposed shipping container, or even a vacant retail space. These unconventional locations can

add an extra element of surprise and
excitement for your guests.

Considering Logistics and Cost

When evaluating potential locations, it's essential to
consider the logistics and costs involved. Here are
some important factors to keep in mind:

1. **Size and Layout**: Make sure the space
   can accommodate your desired number of
   guests and kitchen equipment. Consider the
   flow of your operations and the layout of the
   space to ensure it meets your needs.
2. **Amenities and Facilities**: Assess the
   availability of essential facilities such as
   water, electricity, and ventilation. Depending
   on your menu, you might also need access
   to refrigeration or specialized equipment.
3. **Permits and Licenses**: Check local
   regulations to ensure that the space is
   suitable for operating a pop-up restaurant.
   Make sure to obtain the necessary permits
   and licenses to stay compliant with the law.
4. **Budget**: Determine your budget for the
   location and factor in additional costs such
   as insurance, utilities, and any necessary
   renovations or improvements to the space.

Negotiating Lease Terms

Once you've identified a potential location, it's time
to negotiate the lease terms. Here are some tips to
consider:

1. **Short-term Lease**: Opt for a short-term lease that aligns with the limited duration of your pop-up restaurant. This will give you more flexibility and minimize financial risk.
2. **Rent Negotiation**: Negotiate a fair rent that fits within your budget. You might consider offering a percentage of your revenue instead of a fixed rent, especially if you're unsure about your sales projections.
3. **Clear Terms and Agreements**: Ensure that all terms and responsibilities are clearly documented in a lease agreement. This includes maintenance obligations, insurance requirements, and any special arrangements.

Finding the right location is a critical aspect of starting a pop-up restaurant. By understanding your target audience, conducting thorough research, considering logistics and costs, and negotiating favorable lease terms, you'll be well on your way to finding the perfect spot for your pop-up restaurant. So take your time, do your homework, and get ready to create an unforgettable dining experience!

Chapter 5: Legal and Regulatory Considerations

Starting a pop-up restaurant is about much more than just cooking delicious food and creating a unique dining experience. You must also navigate the legal and regulatory landscape that governs the foodservice industry. In this chapter, we'll explore the essential legal and regulatory considerations you need to address when starting your pop-up restaurant.

Understanding Food Safety Regulations

Food safety should be at the top of your priority list. Ensuring that your food is prepared and handled safely and hygienically is crucial for protecting your customers' health and maintaining a stellar reputation. The first step is familiarizing yourself with local food safety regulations and guidelines, which can vary depending on your location. Here are some key areas to focus on:

Obtaining Permits and Licenses

First, check with your local health department or food safety agency to determine what permits and licenses you need. These might include a food handler's permit, a temporary food establishment permit, or a mobile food vendor license. Make sure you apply for these permits well in advance, as the process can take some time.

Food Handling and Storage

Proper food handling and storage practices are essential to prevent foodborne illnesses. This means maintaining proper temperature controls, practicing good hygiene, and preventing cross-contamination. Train your staff on food safety protocols and regularly inspect your kitchen to ensure compliance.

Regular Inspections

Be prepared for periodic inspections from health department officials. These inspections ensure that your pop-up restaurant meets food safety standards. Keep accurate records, maintain a clean and organized kitchen, and address any issues or violations promptly to pass these inspections smoothly.

Insurance and Liability

Protecting your pop-up restaurant from potential risks and liabilities is essential. Here are some insurance options to consider:

General Liability Insurance

General liability insurance protects your pop-up restaurant from claims related to customer injuries, property damage, or foodborne illnesses. It can cover legal fees, medical expenses, and compensation for damages.

Product Liability Insurance

If you serve food products that could potentially cause harm or illness, product liability insurance is crucial. This type of insurance protects you from legal claims related to foodborne illnesses caused by your products.

Workers' Compensation Insurance

If you have employees, workers' compensation insurance is necessary. It provides coverage for medical expenses and lost wages in the event of an employee injury or illness.

Compliance with Zoning and Licensing Requirements

Pop-up restaurants often operate in unconventional locations like vacant lots, warehouses, or private residences. Ensure you comply with zoning laws and regulations to avoid legal issues. Research local zoning restrictions and seek appropriate permits or variances if needed. Additionally, consider any licensing requirements specific to your pop-up restaurant's concept. For example, if you plan to serve alcohol, you may need to obtain a liquor license. Understand the specific regulations that apply to your business to stay compliant.

Intellectual Property and Trademark Considerations

When creating your pop-up restaurant's brand, logo, and name, think about intellectual property protection and potential trademark issues. Conduct a thorough search to ensure that your chosen name and branding elements are not already registered trademarks. Consulting with an attorney specializing in intellectual property law can help you navigate this complex area.

Conclusion

Understanding and complying with legal and regulatory considerations is crucial for the success and longevity of your pop-up restaurant. By ensuring food safety, obtaining the necessary permits and licenses, securing appropriate insurance coverage, complying with zoning and licensing requirements, and protecting your intellectual property, you'll create a solid foundation for your venture. In the next chapter, we'll dive into marketing and promotion strategies to help you attract customers to your pop-up restaurant.

Chapter 6: Marketing and Promotion Strategies

Marketing and promotion strategies are essential for creating awareness and attracting customers to your pop-up restaurant. In this chapter, we will explore various strategies to effectively market and promote your business.

1. Define Your Target Audience

Before diving into marketing tactics, it is important to identify and understand your target audience. Consider their demographics, preferences, and behaviors to tailor your marketing efforts accordingly. This will help you create relevant and appealing messages that resonate with your potential customers.

2. Create a Strong Brand Identity

Developing a strong brand identity is crucial for standing out in the crowded culinary industry. Your brand encompasses not only your name and logo but also the overall aesthetic, tone of voice, and values. Craft a brand story that engages and connects with your target audience, making them eager to experience your pop-up restaurant.

3. Utilize Social Media

Social media platforms are incredibly powerful tools for promoting your pop-up restaurant. Create engaging and visually appealing content that showcases your menu, ambiance, and unique dining experience. Be active on platforms like Facebook, Instagram, and Twitter to build an online presence, engage with followers, and share updates about your pop-up events.

Pro Tip: Partner with influencers and local food bloggers who have a strong following in your target market. They can help generate buzz and increase visibility for your pop-up restaurant.

4. Collaborate with Other Businesses

Consider collaborating with other local businesses, such as breweries, wineries, or artisanal food producers. By partnering with like-minded businesses, you can tap into their existing customer base and leverage their marketing channels. This cross-promotion can be mutually beneficial and create a win-win situation for both parties involved.

5. Host Tastings and Special Events

Hosting tastings, special events, or pop-up previews can generate excitement and anticipation around your pop-up restaurant. Invite influencers, media representatives, and potential customers to experience a sneak peek of your menu and dining concept. This can create buzz, generate positive word-of-mouth, and attract a crowd for your opening night.

6. Offer Loyalty Programs and Discounts

Rewarding your loyal customers is a great way to encourage repeat visits and build a loyal customer base. Consider offering loyalty programs, special discounts, or incentives for referrals. These strategies not only retain existing customers but also attract new ones through positive word-of-mouth.

7. Optimize Your Website and Online Presence

Ensure that your pop-up restaurant has a professional and user-friendly website. Include essential information such as your menu, location, operating hours, and reservation options. Make sure your website is mobile-friendly, as many customers use their smartphones to search for dining options. Additionally, register your pop-up restaurant on online directories and review platforms to improve your online visibility and reputation.

8. Use Traditional Marketing Channels

While digital marketing is essential in today's age, don't overlook the power of traditional marketing channels. Consider distributing flyers, posters, or business cards in local businesses, community centers, and other high foot-traffic areas. Take advantage of local publications or radio stations to advertise your pop-up restaurant and reach potential customers who may not be active on social media.

9. Collect and Leverage Customer Feedback

Actively seek feedback from your customers and use it to improve your offerings. Encourage customers to leave reviews on platforms like Yelp, Google, or TripAdvisor. Respond to both positive and negative reviews, showing that you value their input. By continuously refining your offerings based on customer feedback, you can ensure a memorable dining experience that keeps customers coming back for more.

Conclusion

Effective marketing and promotion strategies are crucial for the success of your pop-up restaurant. By defining your target audience, creating a strong brand identity, utilizing social media, collaborating with other businesses, hosting special events, offering loyalty programs, optimizing your online presence, using traditional marketing channels, and collecting customer feedback, you can create awareness, attract customers, and build a loyal fan base for your pop-up venture.

Chapter 7: Staffing and Operations

Running a successful pop-up restaurant isn't just about great food and a unique location. It requires careful planning and efficient management of both staffing and operations. This chapter will guide you through the essential aspects of staffing and operations to ensure your pop-up runs smoothly and your customers have a fantastic dining experience.

Organizing Your Team

The first step in staffing your pop-up restaurant is to put together a dedicated and talented team. Think about the key positions you'll need, such as chefs, servers, bartenders, and kitchen staff. The size of your pop-up and the workload you expect will help you determine how many staff members you'll need.

When you start hiring, look for individuals who are passionate about the restaurant industry and align with your concept and vision. Seek candidates with relevant experience and strong interpersonal skills to ensure excellent customer service. Here are some key positions to consider:

- **Head Chef**: The head chef is responsible for menu creation, food preparation, and supervising the kitchen staff.

- **Servers**: Servers take orders, serve food and beverages, and ensure customer satisfaction.
- **Bartenders**: Bartenders prepare and serve drinks, as well as maintain a clean and organized bar area.
- **Kitchen Staff**: Kitchen staff assist chefs with food preparation, cooking, and keeping the kitchen clean.
- **Front-of-House Manager**: This person oversees the dining area, manages reservations, and coordinates the waitstaff.

Training and Development

Once you've assembled your team, it's crucial to provide thorough training to ensure consistency in service and quality. Develop training programs that cover all aspects of your pop-up restaurant, including menu knowledge, customer service standards, and operational procedures. Make sure your staff are trained in food safety and handling practices to maintain a hygienic and safe environment.

Encourage continuous learning by offering opportunities for professional development and cross-training within different roles. Here are some training tips:

- **Conduct Orientation Sessions**: Introduce staff to the pop-up restaurant's concept, mission, and values.

- **Provide Training Manuals and Resources**: Give staff reference materials to help them understand their roles better.
- **Regular Training Sessions and Refresher Courses**: Reinforce knowledge and skills periodically.
- **Encourage Teamwork and Collaboration**: Foster a sense of teamwork among staff members.

Smooth Operations

Efficient operations are key to the success of your pop-up restaurant. Implement systems and processes that streamline daily tasks and ensure a seamless dining experience. Here are some essential operations considerations:

- **Inventory Management**: Use a system to track ingredient and supply levels to avoid running out of critical items during service.
- **Order Management**: Consider using technology, such as tablet-based ordering systems, to increase efficiency and accuracy.
- **Time Management**: Develop a schedule that allows for smooth transitions between meal services and manages staff breaks efficiently.
- **Workflow Optimization**: Design your kitchen and dining area layout to facilitate smooth workflow and minimize bottlenecks.
- **Communication Channels**: Establish clear communication channels between

staff members to ensure effective coordination during service.

Leverage technology and tools to improve operations:

- **Point-of-Sale (POS) Systems**: Modern POS systems can streamline ordering, payment processing, and inventory management.
- **Customer Relationship Management (CRM) Software**: Use CRM tools to manage customer information, track preferences, and provide personalized service.
- **Online Reservation Systems**: Utilize online platforms to manage bookings and minimize wait times.
- **Kitchen Management Software**: Implement software that helps with recipe costing, inventory tracking, and menu planning.

Maintaining a Positive Work Environment

Creating a positive work environment is essential for staff morale and productivity. Treat your team with respect, provide opportunities for growth and recognition, and encourage open communication. Regularly seek feedback from your staff to understand their needs and concerns. Address any issues promptly and implement improvements as needed.

Recognize and reward staff members for their hard work and exceptional performance. A positive work environment not only benefits your team but also enhances the overall dining experience for your customers. Here are some ways to boost staff morale:

- **Employee Appreciation Events and Outings**
- **Incentive Programs for Outstanding Performance**
- **Training and Development Opportunities**
- **Regular Meetings for Feedback and Communication**
- **Supportive and Transparent Management Approach**

Conclusion

Staffing and operations are critical components of running a successful pop-up restaurant. By organizing an efficient team, providing thorough training, optimizing operations, and maintaining a positive work environment, you can ensure a memorable and enjoyable dining experience for your customers. Efficient staffing and operations will contribute to the overall success and longevity of your pop-up restaurant. So, take the time to plan and prepare, and watch your pop-up restaurant thrive!

Chapter 8: Creating an Unforgettable Dining Experience

Creating a memorable dining experience is essential for the success of your pop-up restaurant. It's not just about serving delicious food; it's about crafting an atmosphere and ambiance that leaves a lasting impression on your guests. In this chapter, we will explore various strategies and techniques to help you create an unforgettable dining experience.

Designing the Interior

The design and decor of your pop-up restaurant play a significant role in creating a unique dining experience. Think about the overall theme and concept of your restaurant and reflect it in the interior design. Choose furniture, lighting, and decorations that align with your brand identity and create a comfortable and inviting ambiance. Consider the layout of your space to optimize the flow of customers and staff. Ensure there is enough space between tables for privacy, but also allow for smooth movement. Pay attention to details such as table settings, linens, and music selection to enhance the dining experience.

Imagine walking into a cozy, dimly lit space with warm colors and rustic wooden furniture. The scent of fresh herbs fills the air, and soft jazz music plays in the background. The tables are set with crisp white linens, and each place setting has a small vase with a single fresh flower. These details create a welcoming and intimate atmosphere that guests will remember long after their meal.

Enhancing Customer Service

Customer service is a crucial element in creating a memorable dining experience. Train your staff to be attentive, friendly, and knowledgeable about the menu. Encourage them to engage with customers, offer suggestions, and address any special requests. Personalize the dining experience by getting to know your regular customers and their preferences. Remember their names, food allergies, and favorite dishes. Small gestures, like sending a complimentary dessert or a personalized thank-you note after their visit, can go a long way in creating a lasting impression.

For example, if you have a regular customer who always orders the same dessert, you could surprise them with a complimentary variation of that dessert, or if you know a guest has a food allergy, make sure your staff informs them about new menu items they can enjoy safely.

Innovative Food Presentation

Presentation is key when it comes to food. Surprise and delight your guests with visually appealing dishes that showcase creativity and artistry. Experiment with different plating techniques and garnishes to elevate the overall dining experience. Consider incorporating interactive elements into your dishes. For example, serving a dish that requires the guest to pour a sauce or assemble their own creation can create a memorable and engaging experience.

Imagine serving a dessert where the guest cracks open a chocolate shell to reveal a luscious mousse inside or a dish that comes with a small pipette of sauce for the guest to drizzle themselves. These interactive touches can turn a meal into an experience.

Pairing Food and Beverages

Offering a well-curated selection of beverages to complement your menu can enhance the dining experience. Consider partnering with local breweries, wineries, or cocktail bars to create unique beverage pairing options. Train your staff to provide educated recommendations on pairing food and beverages. Encourage them to share their knowledge and passion for beverages with your guests, providing an immersive experience.

For instance, you could offer a tasting menu with a paired wine for each course, explaining to your guests why each wine was chosen and how it complements the flavors of the dish. This not only enhances the meal but also educates and engages your customers.

Engaging with the Senses

Appeal to all the senses to create a truly unforgettable dining experience. Pay attention to the aromas in your restaurant. Use scented candles or essential oils to create an inviting and pleasant fragrance. Consider playing soft background music that matches the ambiance of your concept. Experiment with lighting to create a cozy and intimate atmosphere. Utilize dimmed or colored lights to set the mood. Enhance the dining experience by incorporating elements like live music, art installations, or even themed events.

For example, a pop-up restaurant with a Mediterranean theme might use essential oils like lavender and rosemary, play traditional Mediterranean music, and decorate with vibrant colors and artwork inspired by the region. These sensory details transport guests to a different place and time, making their dining experience more immersive and memorable.

Collecting and Utilizing Feedback

To continuously improve your dining experience, it is essential to collect and utilize customer feedback. Encourage your customers to provide feedback through comment cards, online reviews, or social media channels. Regularly review the feedback received and identify areas for improvement. Use this feedback to refine your menu, service, and overall dining experience. Engage with your customers by responding to their feedback, showing them that their opinions are valued and taken into consideration.

For instance, if you receive feedback that the portion sizes are too small, you can adjust them accordingly. If customers rave about a particular dish, consider making it a permanent fixture on your menu. By actively listening to and engaging with your customers, you demonstrate that you care about their experience and are committed to making improvements.

Conclusion

Creating an unforgettable dining experience goes beyond the food itself. It requires careful consideration of the interior design, customer service, food presentation, beverage pairing, engaging the senses, and collecting feedback. By focusing on these aspects, you can create a unique and memorable experience that keeps your customers coming back for more. Next, in Chapter 9, we will explore the financial management and budgeting aspects of running a successful pop-up restaurant.

Chapter 9: Financial Management and Budgeting

Managing finances and budgeting effectively are crucial aspects of running a successful pop-up restaurant. As a temporary establishment with a limited timeframe, it is essential to carefully plan and allocate your resources to ensure profitability and sustainability. In this chapter, we will explore the key steps and strategies for financial management and budgeting in a pop-up restaurant.

1. Establish a Financial Plan

Before diving into the financial details, it is important to develop a comprehensive financial plan for your pop-up restaurant. This plan will serve as a roadmap for your business and help you make informed decisions regarding expenses, pricing, and revenue projections. Consider the following components when creating your financial plan:

A. Start-up Costs

Identify all the initial costs associated with setting up your pop-up restaurant. This may include renting a space, purchasing equipment and supplies, legal fees, permits, licenses, insurance, marketing, and branding expenses. Carefully estimate these costs to ensure that you have enough capital to cover them.

B. Operating Expenses

List all the ongoing expenses you will incur during the operation of your pop-up restaurant. This may include rent, utilities, ingredients, staff wages, marketing, maintenance, and other miscellaneous expenses. Monitor these expenses closely to ensure they are in line with your budget and make any necessary adjustments when needed.

C. Revenue Projections

Based on your market research and understanding of your target audience, project your revenue for each day, week, or month of operation. Take into account factors like customer footfall, average spending per customer, and seasonal fluctuations. Be conservative in your projections and periodically compare them to your actual revenue to assess your financial performance.

D. Contingency Plan

Prepare for unexpected circumstances by including a contingency fund in your financial plan. This fund can help cover unforeseen expenses or temporary declines in revenue. Aim to have at least 10-15% of your budget allocated to this fund.

2. Track Expenses and Revenue

Accurate and regular tracking of your expenses and revenue is essential for managing your finances effectively. Create a system to record all your income and expenses, whether it's through accounting software or simple spreadsheets.

Categorize your expenses and revenue streams to gain a clear understanding of your financial health.

3. Monitor and Control Costs

Controlling costs is crucial for maintaining profitability in your pop-up restaurant. Regularly review your expenses and identify areas where you can cut costs or find more cost-effective alternatives. This can include negotiating better prices with suppliers, optimizing your menu to minimize waste, and evaluating staffing levels to ensure adequate coverage without overstaffing.

4. Pricing Strategy

Pricing your menu items appropriately is key to generating revenue and covering your costs. Consider factors such as ingredient costs, labor expenses, overheads, and desired profit margin when setting your prices. Keep an eye on your competitors' pricing, but also take into account the unique value and experience you provide to customers.

5. Cash Flow Management

Cash flow management is crucial for the financial stability of your pop-up restaurant. Ensure that you have enough cash on hand to cover your expenses, especially during slower periods. Implement strategies to improve cash flow, such as offering pre-paid reservations or implementing an efficient payment collection system.

6. Financial Analysis and Reporting

Regularly analyze your financial data to gain insights into the performance of your pop-up restaurant. Generate reports that show key metrics such as revenue, expenses, profit margin, and return on investment. Use these reports to identify strengths, weaknesses, and areas for improvement. This analysis will help you make data-driven decisions and adjust your financial strategies accordingly.

7. Seek Professional Advice

If you are not confident in managing the financial aspect of your pop-up restaurant, consider seeking advice from professionals such as accountants or financial consultants. They can provide valuable insights, assist with financial planning, and help you navigate any complex financial matters.

Conclusion

Effective financial management and budgeting are vital for the success and longevity of your pop-up restaurant. It is important to establish a comprehensive financial plan, track expenses and revenue, monitor costs, implement a pricing strategy, manage cash flow, and regularly analyze your financial performance. By diligently managing your finances, you can optimize profitability and ensure the sustainability of your pop-up restaurant.

Chapter 10: Evaluating Success and Future Opportunities

Evaluating the success of your pop-up restaurant is a crucial step in assessing its performance, making improvements, and uncovering future opportunities. By measuring key indicators and analyzing data, you can gain valuable insights that will guide your decision-making process. Plus, staying open to potential future opportunities will allow your concept to evolve and grow.

Measuring Success

When it comes to evaluating the success of your pop-up restaurant, it's important to consider both quantitative and qualitative factors. Here are some key metrics to track:

Financial Performance

Keeping an eye on your revenue and profit margins is essential to assess the financial viability of your pop-up restaurant. Compare your actual financial results with your initial projections to identify any gaps or areas of improvement. Additionally, analyze your cash flow to ensure you have enough liquidity to cover expenses. This will help you understand if your pop-up is financially sustainable.

Customer Satisfaction

Collecting and analyzing customer feedback is another critical aspect. Use surveys, online reviews, and social media interactions to gather feedback. Pay close attention to comments regarding food quality, service, ambiance, and overall experience. Taking customer feedback into account will help you identify areas for improvement and maintain a high level of customer satisfaction.

Repeat Business and Customer Loyalty

Tracking the number of repeat customers and assessing the effectiveness of your loyalty programs, discounts, and promotions is essential in driving customer loyalty. Repeat business is a strong indicator of customer satisfaction and can significantly contribute to the long-term success of your pop-up restaurant.

Brand Awareness and Online Presence

Monitor the growth of your social media following, website traffic, and online engagement. Assess how effectively you are communicating your brand identity and connecting with your target audience. Investing in online marketing strategies can help increase brand awareness, attract more customers, and generate positive word-of-mouth.

Finding Future Opportunities

Once you have evaluated the success of your pop-up restaurant, it's crucial to explore potential future opportunities for growth and expansion. Here are some areas to consider:

Permanent Location

If your pop-up restaurant has been well-received and financially successful, you might consider transitioning to a permanent location. This move can provide stability and allow you to build a loyal customer base. Conduct market research to identify suitable areas, gather information on commercial real estate options, and evaluate lease agreements.

Collaborations and Partnerships

Explore collaborations with other businesses, chefs, or food-related events to expand your network and reach new audiences. Partnering with complementary businesses can create unique dining experiences and generate additional exposure for your pop-up restaurant.

Special Events and Catering

Consider offering catering services for private events, corporate functions, or weddings. This can be a lucrative revenue stream and a way to showcase your culinary skills to a larger audience. Additionally, organizing special events, such as pop-up dinners or themed nights, can create buzz and attract new customers.

Expanding the Concept

Evaluate the potential for expanding your pop-up concept into different markets or exploring new themes. Conduct market research to understand consumer trends and preferences in other areas. Adapting your concept to different locations or incorporating new themes can attract a broader customer base and create new opportunities.

Franchising or Licensing

If your pop-up restaurant has achieved significant success, you may consider franchising or licensing your concept. This allows others to replicate your concept in different locations while providing you with additional revenue streams. However, careful planning, legal considerations, and comprehensive operational systems are necessary before considering this option.

Conclusion

Evaluating the success of your pop-up restaurant is an ongoing process that requires monitoring relevant metrics, listening to customer feedback, and staying open to future opportunities. By understanding your achievements and areas for improvement, you can continuously refine your concept, deliver exceptional dining experiences, and position your pop-up restaurant for long-term success.

So, keep tracking your progress, listening to your customers, and exploring new possibilities. This will ensure your pop-up restaurant remains vibrant, successful, and ever-evolving.